MW01251207

Precious Moments
We Shared
In Time

Precious Moments We Shared In Time

Cynthia Weathers

Rev. date: 04/25/2013

To order additional copies of this book, contact:
Xlibris Corporation
1-888-795-4274
www.Xlibris.com
Orders@Xlibris.com
125410

Contents

Dedication

To Louis and Florence Collington, what can I say about the two people that steered me in the direction that has enabled me to go on with my life? They taught me how to walk and talk until I was able to do those things for myself. They taught me not to judge people on what I think but to look deep down within me to understand. Dad and Mom gave me hopes that every day will bring on new dreams.

My father, Frank Snider Jr.—he trusted two people to enter his child's life to help nurture her while he kept a close watch. I knew it must have been very hard for him deep down within, but he knew what was best. Thank you for having the wisdom to let go.

To my birth mother, Florence Rebecca Weathers-Alston, thank you for letting your uncle and aunt help give me the tool that was needed in order for me to go through this life's journey.

I look at my sister Betty J. Weathers-Howard just to see the strength she has that kept her going. It is like she had set up this new world to protect her brothers and sisters from any harm. To me, she is that angel that has kept my road lit so I could travel without any danger.

Acknowledgement

The dreams and hopes that were given to me seem like they had vanished into thin air without me getting a chance to complete my many challenges. A group of wonderful people entered into my life to create a light at the end of this tunnel so it could enable me to carry on the work that needed to be done. Thanks to their medical skills that placed hope back into my life. We go through life expecting nothing to happen, but things do occur. The hopelessness sometimes will cloud your way of thinking. I truly believe that we all have these special angels that will take care of our needs. These extraordinary doctors that have been instrumental in the well-being of my life; what can I say to them but thank you all for the endless hours that were given to me in my hours of need. There are many wonderful doctors, nurses, nurse aides, and the entire lab. Technicians made sure that my needs were met. It would take me the rest of my life just to name them all. These are just a few of them: Dr. Robert S. April, my first neurologist; Dr. McMurty, my first neurosurgeon; Dr. Meyer B. Statman, PC; Dr. Harmesh Mittal, my first cardiologist; Dr. Claire L. Keating, pulmonologist; Dr. Robert R. Goodman, neurosurgeon; Dr Michael G. Kaiser, neurosurgeon; Dr. Saadi Ghatan, neurosurgeon; Dr. Shanna K. Patterson, neurologist; Dr. Yousaf Ali, rheumatologist; Dr. Christopher E. Mandingo, neurosurgeon; Dr Mark J. Kupersmith, neuro-ophthalmologist; Dr. Neekianund Kluplateea, gynecologist/surgeon specialist; Dr Shepard D. Weiner, cardiologist; and the neuro-ophthalmology clinic at Columbia Presbyterian. Thanks to this group of wonderful people that still keep this old body together, and may God bless you all.

I Cannot Forget Our Teachers

I cannot forget those extraordinary teachers from Santee Elementary and Lincoln High School. I owe those wonderful teachers for the gift that they placed into my life. They taught me and others how to move through life with our heads held high. The teachings that all of us received from them have created this inner strength that has enabled us to withstand all the mighty storms. I remember when I could not hold my pencil nor read a book they taught me how to. I look back now just to see that their teaching will never fade away; it will stand its own ground. They taught us about our country as well as other countries. They taught us the true meaning of being an American. Like reciting the pledge to our flag and reinforcing the reciting of our prayers. Many of you may be gone but will never be forgotten. Thanks.

All Angels Don't Have Wings

You came in as my angel when I could not see my way through. I often wonder how wide your arms could be spread without causing any harm to you. When I called you, it seems like you were right next to the phone, just waiting for me to call. I lay awake wondering how my sister-in-law made it through. It seems like I took what breath that you were breathing for myself, but, Sis, you never complain. Things that I may not see, hear, or touch, you are there to say its okay, so I move on. When your brothers passed the same year, only seven months apart, Verm, you were that open door that kept me going. The kind words and understanding you gave me helped to heal my wounds. I try to search my soul to see where in the world all that inner strength of yours came from. Your late-night talk with me gave me strength to say tomorrow will be another day and I will make it. I know you have many storms, but nothing seems to ever stop you. We will always stand right next to each other in case one of us might fall. You are one of those special candles that will never blow out. Thank you for building that special room that will keep the memories alive.

Can I Read without My Lamp?

Can I see the fine print that has been steering right in front of my face? Hoping that my lamp would give me all the light I would need to create the many ideas that will come my way. Would the light from this lamp help build the fortress to hide my inner thoughts or take refuge from the many silent nights that I will be facing? I am faced with many things and have known ideas how to react. There are many ways to move on in life. Every time I try to combat my feeling, something always seems to pop up. Could this lamp burn out before all the creating that I must do? It is like the spirit has stepped in to guide my every move overnight without me knowing what happened. Life gave me this lamp to follow, hoping that I would be able to understand the true meaning of what it is all about.

Our Lives Have Many Masterpieces

Think of life as pieces of dreams that we seem to live out each and every day. Our dreams try to show us the direction in which way to go. The mixed emotions seem to get in the way of our thinking. Our soul seems to have traveled from one end to another without seeing the change that might take place. This endless journey will take us deep down into places that we had never been. Our dreams have created a shelter for our future that we can enter into at any given moment. Just looking at the door to hear the sound of keys entering into a locked door seems to have almost faded away. We sit around wondering why holidays still hold that same meaning for us. The simple things that we forget, like not remembering what to buy, but you made sure it was always there for us. Sometimes we wonder if you could just only stop by for a brief moment to help us rebuild our new lives.

The Restaurant Is Our Hideaway

The light has been dimmed to create a feeling that you are somewhere in this wonderful, romantic place. My nerve is at the end, not knowing what the mood would be like. We have been coming to this place for years. Tonight will be a very special one for the two of us. Will he still be able to spot our favorite table with the light being dimmed? Rock Me Tonight was playing the song that will bring out every feeling that may have been locked up for years. In this place, you could leave your soul behind without giving it any thought. Just the atmosphere alone could leave you motionless. A slow movement of his hand could express something that has not been registered in my brain. There will be no eye contact because the light has been dimmed. When he came close, I heard his heart beating very fast; at this moment, I felt maybe I've gone to another place. Our waiter came over to give us our menu. For me, I had already known what I wanted. Would this be our good-bye meal? If I could only look into his eyes, maybe it could explain what the next move will be.

CYNTHIA WEATHERS

What Happened to Our Lives?

My bed is very cold now. My heart has no room for anyone else. My soul has moved on in many directions, but my heart still beats the same. You made this special place for us that sometimes, I just wanted to reach out and touch. The shadow that was left behind gave me the warm feeling that you were still around. There is this blank look in my eyes but not in my heart. It will always cover my heart but not my soul. It is like a rosebud waiting patiently to be opened. Will we ever cross the same path again? We will never get that chance to walk around when the dew is on the ground and see the beauty that has been placed in front of us. I no longer wonder what it might have been. The question is, can I take it to another level? We would never get another chance to sit near a roaring fire nor watch the sun set over the hills. Maybe on a cold night, just having a glass of wine and sharing memories that we held so dear to us. Tears on my pillow seem to have all dried up, but the thought of you still lingers on. I often wonder if your dreams are still the same as the ones you had with me.

How Can I Not See the Beauty in My Life?

Whenever I look around and see all the things that God has given me. The great wisdom was to bring about changes that had occurred in my life. I need not have to stand in front of my mirror to see the greatness that he had bestowed upon me. The challenges are there with all my dreams and hopes; it will guide me through all the danger that may or may not enter into life. Sometimes a person can see some things, but other times, it can be right in front of them; he or she may not realize how deep it could be. I always talk about my many storms. When do I come in from them and create these things that were left for me to do? What are the many challenges that seem to have been locked inside of me? Would I be able to stand in front of a crowd and express myself without wondering if everything had gone well? *Don't place my many thoughts in a glass to see which ones may match your ideas of me.* We all have the same glass, maybe shaped a little different but still hold that same value. Grant me the entire thing that can help others without causing any harm.

CYNTHIA WEATHERS

Can My River Flow into the Mighty Sea?

I can hear the roaring sound of the river that flows deep down into the mighty sea. My eyes are closed, but the echo sound of the river flowing, it seems like it has the same sound like when a drum is beating. Can my spirit be like that river where it could change at any given moment? Is this a dream that would take me back to places once visited as a child? Those rivers have held many wonderful memories in this heart of mine when I was a child. Sometimes these rivers have caused me to wander around aimlessly without knowing where to turn. Can my river be as wide but not so deep? I cry, time after time, but never taken out the time to find out if my river would ever run dry. Is there a place deep down where this river will rest? My soul needed to cover everything that dealt with my childhood. People call it the missing dreams; I call it all the missing hopes. The dreams that didn't have wings to fly are water to move into the mighty sea. These feelings are driving me where I must deal with it right away. Sometimes it causes me to cry at any given moment. They were a part of my life that was hidden from me, buried deep down within my soul.

My Book

Which page in this book will I read tonight that could transport me into another place without me realizing what had transpired? I truly believe there is an inner strength that has been carved into my soul without me being aware of it. The struggle that has sent me into many dark corners wouldn't let me rest. Sometimes I speak of the shadows that have followed me from childhood into an adult and challenge my every thought and movement. It has created many doubts that push things into what I call the maybe or someday corner. Whenever I think things will come to an end, something always shows up. Oh, Lord, can I let go of all the midnight madness? This book causes me to check the depth of my soul and place it into question. I kept moving the pages back and forth to search out things that seem to cover my life. Will the eyes close for a brief moment or two for me to get a little rest? Maybe someday I will be able to move way from the many questions that have taken over my thoughts.

CYNTHIA WEATHERS

Don't Count Me Out Yet

How can I count all my blessing without leaving out someone? God gave me many blessing through other people's ideas about me. When walking around, seeing and hearing all the things that have been placed into my life makes me want to write. The inner strength seems to wrap me into such a free spirit with so much emotion, not knowing where to turn. Can this world of ours grant me the inner feeling that has been locked up inside of me all these years? *May the space that holds my heart and soul together grant me peace of mind?* I see two worlds that were laid beneath my feet; trying to live in both of them, it has made me feel lost. Can the hidden tide keep pulling me down without causing me any harm? The stands that I myself may take could create a little hope and peace that will combat the fear in my heart. There is no looking glass that can help me. Maybe my ideas and feelings could create something that can help others.

God Has Given Me Such a Challenge

What is this challenge that the Almighty has placed in front of me? My sadness has turned into an inner strength that I never thought was there. Peace of mind can restore many things within my life. The writing helps me to relieve the inner pain in my heart. People see you but can't hear you. There are many goals that I myself may not get a chance to do. As long as I can with the help of the Lord, things will work out. There are days when I sit down and things just start to form within my head. Life can be many turns of events that will occur. In life, there is this old ship embedded down on the ocean floor that no one can reach it. Everything on that old ship seems like it was placed there for me to escape from. Is my life a part of that ship that has been anchored for so many years? You gave me those challenges that have taken me so far away. My great challenge is this old body of mine. Will it hold out until some of my creating gets done? Around every corner you have challenged me. Things that have been placed at my feet, you gave it to me. My Creator has kept me from not letting go.

Color Means Nothing to Me

We hold many things in our heart today, and colors seem to have stepped in and clouded our minds. The dreams, hopes, faiths, and other things do not have colors within them. We dream of colors but not what those colors hold for us. Grant me that room full with different colors not of mind but of spirit that will help transcend my message. Separate me from colors of sight and hold me to the colors of soul. Help me to lift my hand up, not to harm but to inspire the best that the Almighty has granted to me. This room is dark and full with many colors. I myself cannot see the colors but know it is somewhere around. Can the thing I see or thought I saw help to remove this unrest that lies within my soul? We always use the phrase "Our Father watches over us." To me, it feels like our colors are watching over us. We tend to judge a man by his color of skin but not the true ability of his work. I try very hard to let my true ability speak for me. Those doors that were closed to me helped to inspire who I am, not who I wanted to be.

Hope Seems to Come My Way

Today seems to have shed a little light on the word *hope*.

You may have seen me in the mirror, wondering where I must go.

The spirit of joy not any way to be founded just the mere thought of hopes.

I may not travel the same road nor challenge the world in the same manner, but the sign of hope seems to follow me around every corner.

The sign of hopes seems to have been placed right into my path.

It seems to have transformed my nights into maybe or lack of hopes.

Please let me sleep a little longer so I can capture some of the hopes that may come into my life.

Why must this true moment slip away from me without reaching out to it?

Splendid as it maybe, hopes cause me to stand back to view the character of life.

The things I hold so dare to me bring in to play how I got here.

My Creator must have known where to place me.

Hopes seem to have transcended from the mere looking at a flower to generate all the beauty that is within.

CYNTHIA WEATHERS

I Am at the Crossroads

Sometimes it is very hard to explain to others who I am. I truly believe it is the candle that keeps burning within my soul; that is who I am. The thoughts that are in my head seem to capture those moments in time. These days, I look back and wonder if there could have been more added to my life? Sadness seems to creep into my life without any warning. Life has offered up many things in which I can grab and hold on to. Could the slow movement of life come in to hover over me and cloud my thoughts? Maybe it is just that little gleam of hope coming through my voice with the bright light shining in my face.

The fear of me not to move ahead has stopped me dead in my track. Is there a sign to let me know how to turn? The trees show me all the change that may occur in my life. Such as the leaves change colors, and the trees lose all their leaves. How come the crossroad hasn't led me to the end yet? Is it my soul or maybe my spirit that would hold things in place for me? Trust me; I am okay.

I Cannot Hold Back

Two days ago, there was some news that had taken me way back. There had been movement into my life that came in and overshadowed some of my hopes. Maybe the light that had been moving toward my universe went slightly dark causing such a shadow for just a brief moment. The inner strength that I am clinging onto is helping me to hold the many characters together. It is like a bee buzzing into my ears with so much excitement. I am on this bus, and something keeps coming after me. The sense of there is many fields of dreams that my soul has not been able to tap into. Fields of dreams that has inspired me to seek out the underlying current that brought me to this place. We look at all tomorrows as another day, but in good conscience, it is the same day with different names.

I Live in My Parents' Shadow

The things you taught me still come true in everything I do and say.

I live not for today; I live for the many tomorrows.

How could I forget about the nights when we sat around that old wood heater, talking about how your day had gone?

I saw my dreams in your eyes, my hope in your voice, my understanding through your work, gave me pride.

Money could not buy nor replace the knowledge that the two of you gave to us.

Whenever I think about the two of you, tears start flowing down my cheeks.

The moment in time was created by the both of you to lead us through life's busy highway.

My many nights have forced me not to think of only today but those many yesterdays.

You let us be children first; that is why today, we have turned out to be wonderful parents like you.

Sometimes life comes in and changes just in a blink of an eye.

We May Not Be Stressed Out

How could our struggle be any different from all mankind?

In many ways they are all the same but just the unique way in how we handle it.

Can it be the inner struggle that keeps us from seeking things or understanding the depth of a situation? Sometimes we look around to see if there is something that can lift our spirits. We may not be able to reach all our goals, but the important ones we may have reached them without being aware. The road that we start may not be the same one that would take us in the direction that we must travel. The hope is still there, but our dreams seem to have transformed into something different than we had not anticipated. Must we go on without finding out if this will work out or what? Can our vision be stressed whereas we cannot relate to those things that are staring back at us? We try to escape by thinking about when will tomorrow come to an end. Maybe we will overcome some of the danger that steer us right into our everyday lives. If we would only let the darkness move away and let the beauty and the sunlight come back into our lives.

CYNTHIA WEATHERS

Keep the Spirit Alive

You will never let me stop dreaming. I try to move away from the many thoughts that seem to creep up into my head. It has taken me through many of life's obstacles and created the inner strength that we often take for granted. Some days I don't know which foot should go next, but these inner feelings keep pushing me forward without me being locked up into my own space. When we were born, this life didn't give us any manual to show the right way in which to move or even a map to guide us through. I lay my hand across this wonderful heart of mine to get the many beats that kept this old body of mine still alive. Not knowing quite well that my yesterday would have been my many tomorrows. What is this spirit of ours that creates what seems to be the mighty torch that we can't let go? It has manifested many things without the understanding of how to handle them. You left me early one morning; at that time, it felt like it was a little senseless in how it was done. In my mind, it felt like the spirit had wings in which it had entered into my space without me having any control over it and just flew away. We dream of seeing you and having those conversations that seem to carry us through the night. Whenever the break of dawn seems to come upon us, everything goes away. It is like a cloud that seems to come in and creates this special moment in time.

"Lantern"

The lanterns that light up into the window, can my best friend see them? You gave me three lanterns for our home so that when the light goes out, the glow will protect me from the dark. Must this lantern light up every dark corner of my home as well as my heart? The glow could be seen for miles. I sit back now, thinking maybe this was the reason why he gave those lanterns so that I could have the warm feeling that he will always be there for me. The lantern is like a light bulb that can be seen in every corner of a room. You can see the magical power that has created many special moments in time. It is like reading a novel with all the adventurers that have been locked up. When he left me, I would light the lantern and place it near the window, hoping that maybe he would stop by. Knowing in my heart that was not going to be, but it didn't stop me from lighting the lantern. There is another lantern; that one has been placed into my heart; no winds, hail, or mighty storms will ever be able to turn it off. You can feel the power of that lantern that gives strength and true meaning to all those inner feelings.

CYNTHIA WEATHERS

Let Me Finish, Please

The walks that I've been taking have left me drained.

There is no scene that my life has not covered.

My nights seemed to have drawn out into days.

Could it be that all my challenges have led me down this dark path?

Please let my wings fly me into the direction where I need to go.

Maybe tomorrow will let me see what those yesterdays have created.

But please let me finish so I can see the beauty that has been left behind.

It seems that the heart has thrown out many things for me to hold on to.

Could I challenge those things that can help me?

Please let me finish. Every hope for tomorrow has released a magnitude of maybes.

My tree may not bend in the direction that it must go, but it still can be bended.

The walks that seem to brighten up my spirit in some way are almost gone.

But just please let me finish.

Life Can Leave You with an Empty Bed

The cover has been pulled up to my neck, but there is still an empty space next to me. Could it be the fear of touching the other side would bring more darkness into my life? Those memories that were once shared seem like they had all dried up. The empty bed has taken on its own life span and left me alone. It is not that warm feeling of comfort that will be there to protect me from all harm. It cannot hold; you are even saying those special things that you were once told. The empty bed stands tall like someone has been standing over you. This bed is very cool and holds no true meaning on how you feel in your dark moments. The night has grown much longer from this empty bed. The ceiling seems like it wanted to rest upon your chest. I keep turning from side to side with my eyes wide open. Will this empty bed draw me into another world of disperse? Maybe my mind has been playing tricks on me. I would like to walk away into a forest of trust me. This empty bed has placed itself right into my life, not knowing how I will survive.

CYNTHIA WEATHERS

Look at Me

There is a mystery in my life that wouldn't let me go. It has taken space in all of my thinking and creates those moments that can be unbearable. The mind can move you into many directions, and making the way back could seem very hard. Today is one of my make-me-or-break-me days. The body has created this wall that puts everything into such a dark place; could I just lay back and let what is being done just happen? What are those things that seem to give me the motivation to overcome those inner thoughts? The thoughts seem to come in around midmorning and would let go until noon. We place things on past experiences and dreams that come overnight to replace what seems to be real. I open up my eyes to what I think is real or what makes sense. The world we live in has laid down many rules but fewer guidelines to follow by. You held me in your arms and never explained to me why I was there. Could it be that you were experiencing some of those same feelings that were entered into my space? Why am I trying very hard not to let go of those inner feeling in order for me to take that giant step?

Mama!

You made me breathe when I did not want to.

You made me think before I spoke.

You showed me how great my dreams could become.

You taught me how to stand out from the crowd.

You let me know how love could be expanded without any harm.

You shared with me your hopes and dreams but still kept reminding me of mine.

Some days, I feel that you have left me in a mist of you can do it without me.

Mama, I can feel the sense that you are still creating things for me to carry on.

CYNTHIA WEATHERS

Daddy!

Daddy, I made it through with all my twists and turns.

The long nights around that old wood heater brought light into my future.

I felt deep down alone when you slipped away from me that summer morning.

Then my life slips away from me for just a brief moment?

My understanding of life, Daddy, you showed me how to be strong.

Daddy, you guide your children through some of life's narrow streets.

Today I can truly say we miss you but still can look back and see you.

"Moonlight"

The moonlight has over taken all the darkness that has entered into this beautiful atmosphere. Just the mere movement causes you to wonder where it is coming from. As I attempted to move quickly, the light seems to transform me. The mere thought of any kind of movement causes the light to move with you. Will this light show me the way back home or keep me moving miles away? It gave you the sense that maybe someone could be watching. The movement of light comes down into your path and reaches out and touches everything in its way. I could feel the gentle pose that was placed upon my neck. It will not harm you but just give you the sense of "I am here. You can trust me." The invitation to its space creates this blankness in your eyes that causes many imaginations. Sweat starts to come down slowly; the heart seems to have picked up an exact beat, and the legs begin to get very weak. Could it be a transformation of something is about to happen? It makes you want to think of what this moonlight has in store for you. Don't let this moonlight of mine wander aimlessly without capturing its bare essence of eternal hope.

My Forest Has Many Trees

This forest of mine covers my entire life. It starts from childhood and still continues on. I often wonder how many trees will be cut down before everything will fall into place. Can my writing create that light brush that will help my forest to expand? In the winter, the forest has no leaves, but to me, there is no winter in my forest. The creating part for me never stops; just the mere joy, peace of mind will always be there for me. Could I capture all that beauty this forest has offered to me? My soul needs all the timbers as well as the roots in order for my trees to withstand the many storms and fires that come its way. The forest has an inner sight into my past and future. Sometimes I wonder how often my trees could bend back and forth without breaking. In many ways, that's how my life seems to work. The forest is just there to create that moment in time where everything comes and goes.

My Life Has Changed

I don't know where my mind nor where my soul will rest.

Somewhere, there has been a change in me.

There are many mountains that I may not get a chance to climb or even to challenge.

But somewhere, there has been a change in me.

Can my past memories and present come together and create this refuge for me without causing me to wander around for years, not knowing where to turn?

I truly believe somewhere there has been a change in me.

My thoughts have transformed me into two persons; the different feelings have caused me to question every movement that I must make.

Somewhere, there has been a change in me.

Will the spirit that holds this body together keep watching over my soul?

Lord knows there has been a change in me.

My thunderstorms are whenever I sit at the computer and just write about all the beautiful things that I can still see and hear.

Somewhere, there has been a change in me.

Sometimes there are many shadows that seem to follow me around or things that call self-doubt, that cause my mind to drift.

Somewhere, there has been a change in me.

Whenever I walk into one room to another and feel the warmth that was left behind from my best friend, lover, and husband (Larry), then at that moment,

I truly believe there has been a change in me.

My Mirror Has No Glass

Is it an image of my soul that has been wandering, not knowing where to turn? I sit at my computer and just write about all sorts of things. Sometimes the image comes through with such power that it causes me to think for a very long time. In a brief moment in time, my mind has carried the many thoughts back and forth like whenever the tide comes in and goes out. Will I be able to let my tears flow when the time comes? My childhood has left me with many questions that I don't have any answers for at this time. The mirror wouldn't let me go. This mirror has showed me things that I would not have given any thought to. Like the true blessing that we hold dear to our heart. Our spirit is like that mirror that has reflected all the images that we cannot understand. Like my parents leaving us without saying good-bye. Everyone thinks that they have a good hold on that mirror, but how could they without the understanding of how the mirror works?

CYNTHIA WEATHERS

My Roses Need No Water

Whenever I think of my roses, I always think of you. The many colors that you gave me create the confident to withstand the world that you left behind. Sometimes I wonder if you understood what the different colors meant to me. You may have gone away from me, but I can still see all these different colors of roses you gave to me. Down to the long stems and different fragrances that flow into the air help to create these moments that will last forever. I may not get a rose on my pillow or even in a vase, but it will always be in my heart. It is like a treasure that we know is there but could not ever be found. Can I trust my heart to let go so others may see the different colors of roses that you gave to me? Sometimes I feel that holding my roses so tightly may cause them to die. The last bunch you gave to me, it was placed in a book that we loved to read. How could I not see in my darkest hours what those roses had meant to me? The smells seem to travel with me into every corner of my life. It is like how the moonlight reaches down and captures all the beauty in a given space. At that moment, could it be that the smell of those roses and the moonlight brought all the magic back into my life again? *Please just let my roses bring some kind of comfort to others like they have done for me.*

My Trees Could Not Hide the Beauty of the Waterfall

Overlooking that beautiful mountain nestled between those trees; you can see such a magnificent waterfall. As we walk toward the waterfall, you can hear the sound of water cascading down the mountainside with breezes blowing in your face. The mere beauty can cause your mind to wander around to escape whatever you may have left behind. At the bottom, there lies this beautiful stream where a person could place their foot into. Today, the temperature has reached 90 degrees; you would have never known with the waterfall coming down. The time has come for me to leave; would some of these memories travel back with me? The waterfall has brought back those moments in time when our parents would take us into the forest just to see the thing that Mother Nature had bestowed upon us. To escape from the everyday life, to see, hear, and smell things that the nature walks had given to us could make a person just want to stay and never leave.

CYNTHIA WEATHERS

Our Log Cabin Will Still Be Ours

Today will be the first time that my heart will let me revisit our log cabin. Nestled deep in the woods lies our beautiful log cabin. My thoughts sometimes wanted to hold me back from the gray area that was left in my heart. There were many long walks that we once had taken. Sometimes those walks would leave me very drained, but I would go on. There were paths that I felt Mother Nature had carved out just for the two of us. To see all the wonderful things that our log cabin has brought to us, like waiting to watch the sunset with you, helped to create something special that would stay with me for a lifetime. The bright-orange color setting of the sun coming through the trees helped to light up the pathway where your eyes could see for miles. In the early morning, you could see all the different kinds of animals coming close to our log cabin. The fresh morning air would leave you breathless. Somewhere near, it sounds like people are working. A few days later, I saw where they were cutting down some of the timbers. My heart wanted to stop just for a second or two, not knowing if our beautiful hideaway will be there next year. The smells from the ham, bacon, biscuits, and eggs with the brewing of fresh coffee came flowing from out the kitchen. Maybe it will not be such a good day for that special walk into the woods. It will take us three miles away from our log cabin where there is a beautiful brook cascading down the mountainside. Wildflowers had already started to bloom right at the edge of the mountainside; to me, it looks like a good spot to enjoy our lunch. Being here with you had an airy feeling; maybe we could just stay here forever? Our log cabin will always be a special place where everything will remain the same. Good night, sweet dreams, cupcake!

Someone Has Been Watching Over Me

Looking back now to see how far the magic has healed the empty space in my life. I hold my head up and look toward the heavens to see if someone has been looking down on me. Never did I expect that all my angels had their wings on, flying all over me. Today, it feels like there were no words; only time had taken its place. These emotions came in like whirlwinds and moved everything that stood in my way. I stood near the sea to feel that entire ocean breeze come rowing in, hoping that someone would row in and capture me. Must I take these few precious moments and not think of me, just think of how you set me free?

CYNTHIA WEATHERS

Surrounded by Pain and Guilt?

What is wrong with pictures? I cannot see nor understand the true meaning of what is going on? People talk to each other but, less than five minutes, talk about each other. I walk around, trying to see all the beauty that Mother Nature has bestowed upon us and often wonder what went wrong. That is why I am writing to keep my mind intact. Can we just sit back and see the beauty in all of us? My hurt and need are no different from yours. The love I shared with a friend or my family members is the same as yours. *Please do not paint me because of what you think are how you feel. My brush has already been dipped down in paint, and my understanding of who I am may be much different from what you think.* Will I be able to bring the two souls that were left behind together without causing any damage to me?

Fall Has Arrived Again

I can see the leaves that are falling from the trees. The skies have that orange look that you know summer is all over and the winter is just around the corner. This is the time of year that all the wonderful things seem to happen. The daydreams seem to come very often now. All the wonderful holidays will soon be approaching. The leaves will change from color to color—orange, brown, yellow, red, and rust. When the sun comes shining through the trees, every color gives a sense that you have landed in a magical place. It will make you want to take a nature walk just to see those splendid colors. Standing on my back porch with a cup of hot chocolate, looking at a distance as far as my eyes will let me, it was amazing. Mother Nature has challenged our mere existence to this wonderful world. Am I reading too much in this or being overwhelmed that I can hardly think? Sometimes the mind tends to play tricks on you. The fall was also a romantic time where we would take a drive in the country to check out all the different kinds of foliage. While you were driving, in a brief moment, I catch you taking a glance at me. You're gone out of this world, and I am hoping that the same beautiful foliage is there with you. One day, I happened to look up toward the heaven and asked the Almighty if he could grant me just a few moments with the man that I still adore. Maybe take the last drive in the country to enjoy some of the wonderful foliage. You left me with this special moment in time that will replace all the loneliness within my heart.

The Fireplace Makes Me Feel Alive

My fireplace will burn all night until the morning light. I lie on my back facing the roaring fire, trying to capture the bare essence of all the beauty that could leave a person spellbound for hours. The mystical magic comes in the room and causes the flames to draw me near. Each flame brings out such a feeling; where will we go tonight? Through all its blazing flames, it brings out those romantic feelings. It gives warmth, beauty, and magical power—something that was placed here without a true meaning of its beauty. It can transform your soul, spirit, and mind into an unforeseeable danger. The exotic feeling that you experience can alone cripple into your most inner thoughts. The light was turned off, and the curtain at the window was pulled back to let the moonlight enter the room; at that moment, my heart felt like it wanted to skip a beat. Would I ever be able to recover from the magical power it has captured in my mind as well as my soul?

My thoughts seem to wander into many directions. It seems like you are in a time capsule without any hopes of returning. My thought is still traveling, hoping that the snow will soon arrive. Then suddenly, looking through my window, I caught a glimpse of that special person carrying what looked like a dozen roses and maybe a bottle of wine. I am hoping that he would enjoy some of those special moments with me. I open up my door, hoping that he would see the gleam in my eyes that could transport into a different time zone. Soon he would have his arms around me. Holding me gently although the light was turned off, I could see the gleam in his eyes from the fireplace. The fireplace has given the room such a romantic feeling. I could tell by the way he held me so closely to him that my fear had melted way. If this was a dream, I didn't want to wake up. Those moments for me were breathtaking. At that moment, I had no thoughts, but many questions: had our bodies being transferred to another place? The fireplace scene has taken control over every part of our bodies as well as our minds, hearts, and souls. Ten minutes later, after he entered my home, we walked toward the window and saw the snowflakes starting to slowly come down. Then all of a sudden, the sky became very dark and the snow was getting heavier and heavier I could not believe what was happening; it seemed like the heaven had opened up and swallowing the both of us. The life that we knew had suddenly come to a complete stop . . . He held my hand while we walked toward the fireplace. I would always treasure those moments of uncontrollable feelings that have given me hope. He places another log on the fire, and you could hear the popping sound. Then we lay down in front of the fireplace, watching every colorful display. I truly believe the magic from the fire had placed us into another state of mind. Minutes later, he got up and walked toward the table to get two glasses of wine. At that moment, I didn't want the evening to ever end. The warmth of the fire and his head lay on my lap while we both sipped on wine turn out to be an enjoyable night. Our souls seem to have captured all the mystical magic. The soft touch of his hands caused me to fall into an unconscious state. Tonight, the fireplace has made slaves out of us.

There Is a Misty Look in Your Eyes

My life has created this mask that reminds me of the thoroughly misted eyes of yours. How could I have captured such a magnificent part of you without causing my life to come into the cross fire? There were days when I walked around, not knowing which avenue to take, just the mere thought of those misty eyes of yours. Sometimes I think that the heaven must have opened the doors to create all the colors that seem to draw me into a spin. Some people talk about the mist in the sky that blocks the sunlight from their view, but I talk about your misted eyes that transformed me into unforeseeable beauty. It had control of my mind whereas I could hardly think. It felt like all the magic had left me, just the mere thought of your warm body that had left me dangling. Oh, how I harvest the mind and soul in our past life that will carry me forth into my new life. Can I still plant the seed of beauty that was left at my footsteps without causing me to stumble? The picture on my wall will not give justice to those misted eyes of yours.

There Is No Strangeness in Here

Whenever darkness comes, it can color the hopes and unforeseeable dreams. There can be no anger, just the mere emptiness that was left inside. We look for many helping hands that were supposed to be there for us. How could those eyes miss that many signs? It seems that life had shown us one thing and granted us another. We felt that something had opened up all the wounds, and nothing came in to heal or remove the debris. Our challenge in this life was to overcome the obstacle that may cross our path. Every corner we turn the strange shows up to create a giant pitfall. How could the childhood dreams turn out to be the adult nightmare? The stranger never leave us at any given moment; it just controls whatever life has to offer us. Can we stop and think maybe the strange are our ideas of who we should be instead of who we are in life? The magnates that draw us from our hopes and dreams of being someone else can stop us from achieving our goal. I may not climb the ladder the same way you do, but I can still climb.

CYNTHIA WEATHERS

This Poem Is to Our Parents

Our parents didn't dampen our spirit.

Just gave us the will to climb.

The two of them didn't take away who we were.

They gave us the strength to move ahead.

Dad and Mom didn't try to control our minds nor our souls.

They just set forth a vision that we had to challenge.

The two of them didn't shorten our steps.

They just enabled us to make giant steps.

They taught us what dignity, trust and faith were all about—the most powerful things.

Dad and Mom gave us their love and respect.

Waves

These waves have embarked upon my soul without letting any strangeness enter into my life. It has placed me into situations that sometimes I don't have any control over. Sometimes it feels like a wave is coming to drag me far away. Having no idea where my soul will land causes me to move with caution. These waves have left many souls behind, lost in those uncharted waters. Whenever I look up, it seems like this huge mountain of water coming over me just to crush my soul, leaving no doubt in my pathway that may encounter this fear of mine. In those waves, there is nothing to hold on to but the idea that it will come over me with such a power that will challenge my every being. My mind has been wondering how I could withstand this pressure of excitement without seeing where I am going. Let's just move the page up a little farther and let this true moment in time hammer its way through. Maybe those waves could guide me through to what may be lying ahead for me.

We Will Never Stand Alone

Our souls seem to have passed this way before without wondering who we may become. We stand on solid ground, not knowing how we got here. The inner strength that we share created this world for others to see, and hope that they too will become a part of it. My space may not be the same as yours, but my hope is known differently from yours. *All the shadows that you may have cast upon us is not ours alone; it is like an inner strength that causes us to step back into time for only a brief moment.* Whenever I look at myself, what I see is just a mere image of a thousand faces staring back at me. These thoughts of mine have opened up, and then I will take a part in all the challenges that may be placed upon my shoulder. Our souls have come together without any understanding about the many tasks we will face. Every branch that falls from a tree may not get destroyed. My branch may have something that someone could hold on to for just a brief moment. It is like us holding on for that last dream. Can we create a moment in time without causing any harm to someone else? Please don't let the many branches from our trees get lost without knowing what it could have created.

When Do I Know That Everything Is All Right?

Sometimes it feels like the whole world is against me, but I know it is well with my soul. The need to know has created my unsolved issues that seem to have centered on my past history. Will the doors stay open in my lifetime and grant me all the grace that the Almighty had bestowed upon me? Can there be that many shadows that have been hovering over my head? My space seems to be very small, but the work that I was placed here to do has become gigantic. Everyone has their own ideas of what they will perceive our life to be. The mailman has arrived; will the answer be with him? Whenever I look back now, will the joys of all those yesterdays help me to live the rest of my life with a little peace of mind? I think about the many fields of dreams that had entered into my lifetime without realizing how I made it through. Will my tomorrows bring about all those things that still need to be challenged in my life? When I get up in the morning things are still the same. I can still dress myself, still have both legs; my vision in both eyes is still here. The mere joy of being able to say good morning has brought joy to my soul.

When Do We Ever Stop Crying?

We shared many tears that can bring all the walls crumbling down. How can we stand around and miss all the feelings that have been left behind? Our emotions seem to center around not just us but the whole world in which we live in. Judge us not because of our outer appearance but our ability to create an inner peace within our souls. Let our eyes be the tools that will help to heal our many wounds. Let no man create what they think we should become. Our tears will dry up one day and be replaced with a peace of mind.

When?

When did I learn that my challenge in life would take me down this path?

When did I learn how the both of you were so special to me?

When you show me how to walk, talk, dress myself, and told me the first day at school was not going to be bad. When I graduated from high school, then I realize that the hardest thing for me to do was leaving home to start my new life.

When did I realize that the two of you were my treasures, with all the gold I would ever need for the rest of my life?

When I sat down and listened to all the wonderful things that the both of you had in store for me.

The both of you taught me not to judge others by looking at them but by the inner spirit that they showed to me.

You taught me how to capture all those *when* without forgetting my inner spirit as well as my soul.

No one can touch the word *when*, but you can hear and see those *when*.

I truly believe that's why the gift of *when* came into our lives.

Let my when be my when but also let it be the many when that can create a moment in time for all of us.

Will the Light Ever Turn Off?

Sometimes the light seems to have cast a spell over me. The words kept coming; it is like turning on that old faucet. What a creative mood I seem to have gotten myself caught in. You spared me no room for what it may have been. Just those lights that have me tied up into knots. Could it be those blind spots that kept coming back to me? In winter, the trees lose their leaves, but in the spring, they come back like nothing had ever happened. I seem to drift off into a space-like world, trying to hold on to that inner magic. Deep down, my soul tries to fight with those bright lights shining into my soul. But there has always been this fire that lights up the door to my heart. I feel like the light may crash some of those moments in time without me knowing when. Maybe one day all my faith would come in and show me that wonderful way through all the darkness whenever the light gets turned off.

Will You Be My True Valentine?

I will light those candles and think of the moment that you would enter into our space. Just the mere thought that you may be right around the corner sends chills down my spine. What must I wear to help create this moment in time? Maybe the petals of red roses that travels from my doorway across the floor and land all over my bed? Could it be a bottle of champagne being chilled in our favorite bucket? The moonlight from the window will give the room such a spectacular feeling of its own. The man of my life has surrendered every inch of his soul that has left me wandering around, lost into space. It seems to have created a magic that you may have read in one of those romantic novels. At this moment, my soul seems to vanish into another time zone. I need not question myself on every movement because the power of my spirit has taken control of all my senses. The belief that the two of us have created such a moment in time that will enable us to transcend those feelings over our lifetime.

CYNTHIA WEATHERS

Wintry Blues

Oh, how could I sleep tonight, listening to that wintry blues? The whistling sound of the wind and darkened sky seem to create an airy feeling that something will soon be coming. I often wonder if this season was just made for two lovebirds like us. To cuddle up into this old worn blanket, sipping a cup of hot chocolate with a special friend and listening to the old-time blues. Oh, these wonderful, beautiful wintry nights just waiting for that first cascading of snowy flights. The darkened sky has turned all gray, and the brisk winds with the moonlight have struck a pose right on the windowsill. To let you know that Old Man Winter will soon be in. There is no sound of any traffic that you could hear for miles. The cold wind seems to have entered into every corner of my inner thoughts. Once again, Mother Nature has wily created another thing of spectacular beauty. Just to see the beautiful white snowflakes flowing from the sky like feathers that could even light up a child's eyes. It seems like every snowflake has it own mind to create, something that could keep a person in suspense or maybe lose their mind. The daydream kept coming and coming of just being a child playing in the drifting snowflakes with his friend and a dog. We were faced with who could build the tallest snowman. I am hoping that the snow wouldn't come down so heavy until the snowmen were finished. Oh, this has been a wonderful ending to such a magnificent day . . .

You Never Let Me Forget Who I Am

Let no man try to create a world for you. You step in and open the space into my life that causes me to wonder how it would be. The things that my life comes in contact with or even the many challenges that seem to come in every day haven't stopped me yet. The shelter that was made by your hand seems to have placed me right into the center of everything. You gave me grace, faith, hope, and plenty of love that sometimes I truly believe that the many questions I ask myself every day keep me from not heading in the wrong direction. Sometimes I could feel the touch of your hand helping me along life's busy highway. Without a word, that gentle, warm breeze came blowing across my face, and I knew you were near. Whenever my tears start to flow, you step in and say, "Not now, my child, there is more work that needs to be done." I see many holidays come and go just to be faced with the knowledge that you have created this heavenly body that I may get the opportunity to wake up to see each and every day.

Can the World Strip Me from All My Pride?

Whenever I see little children from other countries stripped of their rights, tears start flowing down my cheeks. The mere thought of whom I am, that my life is not like a piece of property waiting for someone to rescue me. It seems like my soul has been locked up in prison from the years of living in fear. I may be able to create those things that can help remove the blind spots that have hovered over me. Oh, strengthen my mind and begin to heal all my inner feelings. Create the time where I may go out and just challenge this world of ours. Please don't take away my ideas, trust, and faith; just let me be me! The world may wash me down, but my pride will never fade away. I will not let my pride overtake me where I myself cannot comprehend what this life can be. The room in my heart that I need to expand sometimes causes me to move in the wrong direction. The moment in time will give me the tranquility that will transform my soul.

Today Has Landed Me into Hell

Sometimes I often wonder, had I ever crossed this line before without any ideas about how to get back? My soul has lost many hours of wondering; will this be the day everything will come together? We talk about everything but never come to a true understanding of how it works. The danger I see in front of me cannot explain the feelings that will linger on. Life could be as cruel like most of us think it is. My day starts out like any another day with a few obstacles. One call after another, sometimes I get the feeling where do things go from here. Can I extend my love far enough so others could reach it? My cries seem to have fallen on deaf ears. At times, I feel like I'm losing my sense of being. People come to you with arms wide open, not knowing what to expect. Will there be anyone to listen for a moment or two, concerning the problem that has taken over me? Maybe the door will close very tight, and no one will be able to get through. I can see the sun is almost down; hoping tomorrow will stand its own ground.

CYNTHIA WEATHERS

Don't Challenge My Heart or My Soul, Just My Mind

My greatest challenge in life was the loss of both parents less than a year apart. Life is like a light that we know it can be turned off without notice at any given moment. The loss that occurred in such a short period had created a hole within my heart as well as my soul. I kept trying to trace what had happened to me. Can I trust myself to hammer out those feelings that have been buried, and all the mistrust that life had thrown my way? The mind has created many obstacles in my life that wouldn't let me move on are take chances. Like taking a bus ride, talking to a friend, or having just a conversation, then suddenly the feeling that I must write not late but now. My sight may go, my heart may ache, but my writing will take me way back in time where I can share some of my deepest feelings. The direction where my mind will take me to is like a ship that is lost at sea but will find its way back to port.

I Wouldn't Let Go of the Love We Shared Together

There is something very strong that is holding me back where I can't let go. The feeling of joy, peace of mind—oh Lord, those inner feelings seem like they are going to take control of my mind. How could I close those doors, even the one that I did not get a chance to open with my husband, Larry? Please tell me, oh LORD how can I do it? My soul has created a sense of where do I go from here. You are gone, and the feeling still lingers on. Sometimes we sit down to see or hear what is being said, but the sadness can overtake us at any given moment where nothing seems to make any sense. Please don't stand and just look at me and wonder what is wrong. Stand by my side, and just listen to me. I may not cry out loud, but the tears are still there all locked up inside. How could my world, at this moment in time, be so confusing? The many times you held me and took care of our needs will help me through all my darkest moments. I often wonder what it is like for you being there. *We had created those moments in time that nothing or no one could tear apart.* Sometimes I can feel that special touch or think about the look in your eyes that kept me wanting to go on. The memories of you will always be in my heart as well as in my soul. To a wonderful man I adore Larry.

CYNTHIA WEATHERS

Our Pillows Need No Covers

The years have passed since you were gone, but lying on those pillows with all the smell still lingers on. Lying there has engulfed my whole being. Will these feelings move me away from the world that I must create for myself? When I lay my head down, it feels like you are right next to me, breathing every breath of mine and challenging my every thought. Sometimes I could hear the soft words that you spoke gently into my ears.

That makes me wonder if you are still near. How could it be the mere thoughts of this could make a person go insane? Maybe if I would get rid of those pillows, then my thoughts of you will leave forever. His teardrops are still there from the time he cried without me being aware of what was going on. I do believe if they could say something, they would say that he still loves me. The smell of your sweat that was left behind on those pillows, I will never be able to wash it out. Some people talk about an out-of-body experience that can captivate the unimaginable things that no one could explain. The pillow has no word that can say hello or have any answer to your problems. Just your willingness to lie there and having those thoughts flowing through your head can fill in the empty moment that was left inside. My nights have known challenge; it is the morning dew that keeps me wondering what to do.

Maybe These Arms of Mine Need Someone to Hold

Every day I wake up knowing well that I will never have those loving arms of yours to hold me. The whole world seems to just move on without looking back to see if I am okay. Those precious moments come and go like the dreams we have of that special someone being here. Can we make some kind of sense out of what has happened in our lives? Sometimes when I hear the song of yesterday playing, it brings back the true meaning of how things used to be. Will we sit back and see all our yesterdays turn out to be our many tomorrows? I cannot foresee what may be ahead of us but the door being slightly jarred open so that we may be able to come in whenever the road gets a little rough. If you would allow that wonderful person to enter into your space, it may create something of beauty. The love that you brought into our life has helped me to wake up each and every morning. Could the songs remove the everyday stress that has challenged my life? Those many love notes that were left behind, maybe they can cause you to think about what the next move will be.

CYNTHIA WEATHERS

My Two Worlds May Have Come Together

Sometimes I often wonder if some of my great-grandfathers and great-grandmothers left a part of their lives behind for me. The many things that have accompanied me in this life have created heartaches. Around every corner, it felt like a part of them may be standing right at my foot. I know that my strength has been weakened by so many ups and downs, but there are these voices that help to maintain the true balance in my life. Those rocks that I may hide my true feelings behind cause me to have many doubts about my capability within me. Their past lives felt like they had entered into my life. I see things that have no meanings whatsoever to my life. The mirror that has no glass created a link between two worlds. There are days when my thoughts had transformed me back into a different time. Maybe the old Negro songs have planted their shadows into my space with such a force. It had incorporated the generation of where our lives start and how it may end. Has my inner spirit got caught in been this two world and wouldn't let go.

The Ocean Breeze Has Placed Me into a Wonderful Frame of Mind

Lying across my bed, feeling the warm breeze coming across my body left no doubt in my mind. This ocean breeze comes in like a storm that leaves nothing untouched. The different smells that blow in with it create a sense of being on a boat sailing around the islands. Will I take the time to enjoy these precious moments or just let them fade away without giving them any thoughts? Deep down, I can sense something has happened to my soul that has led me down this path. The curtains at my windows seem to have taken on a life of their own from the breeze blowing back and forth. I have measured every movement and all my thoughts that have entered into this space. This ocean breeze will not let go; it just keeps holding on to all its power that has stirred up those emotions inside of me. Sometimes you can feel and hear the many different winds coming through the windows without even moving a muscle. The hopes that this may last all day and night could lead you to believe that your soul has wandered off into a foreign space. I am floating high above, right into the clouds, not knowing if I might fall through; it makes me still want to float. I feel that my spirit has been creating this moment for many, many moons now.

This Morning, the Snow and Ice Never Stop Coming Down

Oh, what a wonderful sight to behold—just the mere thought of seeing all those snowflakes and ice hitting against my windows. Then my thoughts seem to have taken me through many adventurous places. This kind of weather could bring out all sorts of imaginations, like seeing me sliding down a hill that has been covered with mountains of snow. It seems like the sky had brought out its own musical treats and settled them right outside my window. It has also brought back many childhood memories. To me, the sense of how old I am didn't even enter into my head; just the memories of being a child kept coming back and forth. I truly believe that the falling snowflakes flowing endlessly down from the sky have captured those romantic moments. I didn't want to light this fire because my special someone was no longer here with me. The light from the fireplace will give off a glowing feeling to this atmosphere. Sometimes I wonder if Larry is getting the same romantic feeling that has engulfed me. Only those daydreams seem to come in this type of weather. Oh, let not my spirit wander, but let my spirit flow freely.

CPSIA information can be obtained at www.ICGtesting.com
Printed in the USA
LVOW061003100713

342103LV00002B/94/P

9 781479 784844